W9-AYO-143

# Harriet Beecher Stowe

### By Mary Hill

Welcome Books™

Children's Press®
A Division of Scholastic Inc.
New York / Toronto / London / Auckland / Sydney
Mexico City / New Delhi / Hong Kong
Danbury, Connecticut

Photo Credits: Cover, pp. 11, 19 © Hulton/Archive/Getty Images; pp. 5, 17 © Bettmann/Corbis; pp. 7, 21 Library of Congress Prints and Photographs Division; p. 9 the Schlesinger Library, Radcliffe Institute, Harvard University; p. 13 Library of Congress Rare Book and Special Collections Division; p. 15 © Historical Picture Archive/Corbis
Contributing Editor: Jennifer Silate
Book Design: Daniel Hosek

Library of Congress Cataloging-in-Publication Data

Hill, Mary, 1977-
   Harriet Beecher Stowe / by Mary Hill.
   p. cm. — (Real people)
   Includes index.
   Summary: A biography of the nineteenth-century author whose anti-slavery novel "Uncle Tom's Cabin" helped intensify the disagreement between North and South.
   ISBN 0-516-25865-6 (lib. bdg.) — ISBN 0-516-27887-8 (pbk.)
   1. Stowe, Harriet Beecher, 1811-1896—Juvenile literature. 2. United
States—History—Civil War, 1861-1865—Literature and the war—Juvenile
literature. 3. Authors, American—19th century—Biography—Juvenile
literature. 4. Abolitionists—United States—Biography—Juvenile
literature. 5. Antislavery movements—United States—Juvenile
literature. [1. Stowe, Harriet Beecher, 1811-1896. 2. Authors, American.
3. Abolitionists. 4. Women—Biography.] I. Title. II. Series: Real
people (Childrens Press)

PS2956.H55 2003
813'.3—dc21

                                                                    2002153942

# Contents

Meet Harriet Beecher Stowe.

Harriet was a **writer**.

4

5

Harriet Beecher was born in 1811.

She lived in **Connecticut**.

7

Harriet Beecher **married** Calvin Stowe in 1836.

**9**

There was **slavery** in some parts of America when Harriet was alive.

She thought slavery was wrong.

Harriet wrote a book about slavery.

It was called *Uncle Tom's Cabin.*

UNCLE
# TOM'S CABIN.
BY
### HARRIET BEECHER STOWE.

WITH

*Twenty-seven Illustrations on Wood*

BY

## GEORGE CRUIKSHANK, ESQ.

EVA AND TOPSY.

LONDON:
JOHN CASSELL, LUDGATE HILL.
1852.

*Uncle Tom's Cabin* told people about how hard life was for **slaves**.

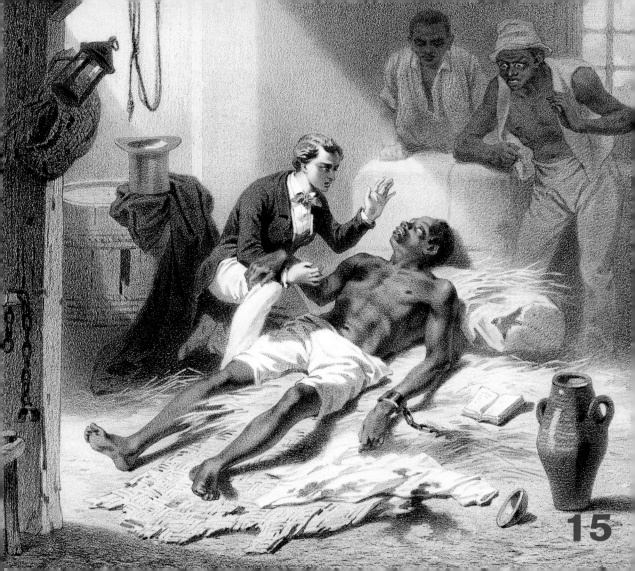

15

Many people read *Uncle Tom's Cabin*.

The book helped to show people that slavery was wrong.

135,000 SETS, 270,000 VOLUMES SOLD.

# UNCLE TOM'S CABIN

# FOR SALE HERE.

AN EDITION FOR THE MILLION, COMPLETE IN 1 Vol., PRICE 37 1-2 CENTS.
" " IN GERMAN, IN 1 Vol., PRICE 50 CENTS.
" " IN 2 Vols., CLOTH, 6 PLATES, PRICE $1.50.
SUPERB ILLUSTRATED EDITION, IN 1 Vol., WITH 153 ENGRAVINGS,
PRICES FROM $2.50 TO $5.00.

## The Greatest Book of the Age.

*Uncle Tom's Cabin* helped to stop slavery.

Harriet wrote many other books, too.

She became a **famous** writer.

Harriet Beecher Stowe will always be **remembered**.

**21**

# New Words

**Connecticut** (kuhn-**net**-ih-kuht) a state in the northeast part of the United States

**famous** (**fay**-muhs) being known by many people

**married** (**mar**-eed) having a husband or wife

**remembered** (ri-**mem**-buhrd) having something in your mind and not forgetting it

**slavery** (**slayv**-uh-ree) the practice of owning another person

**slaves** (**slayvz**) people who are owned by other people

**writer** (**rite**-uhr) someone who writes

# To Find Out More

**Books**
*Harriet Beecher Stowe*
by Robert E. Jakoubek
Chelsea House Publishers

*Harriet Beecher Stowe and the Beecher Preachers*
by Jean Fritz
The Putnam Publishing Group

**Web Site**
**Harriet Beecher Stowe Center**
http://www.harrietbeecherstowecenter.org/life/
This Web site has a lot of information about the life and
times of Harriet Beecher Stowe.

23

# Index

**About the Author**
Mary Hill writes and edits children's books.

**Reading Consultants**
Kris Flynn, Coordinator, Small School District Literacy, The San Diego County Office of Education

Shelly Forys, Certified Reading Recovery Specialist, W.J. Zahnow Elementary School, Waterloo, IL

Sue McAdams, Former President of the North Texas Reading Council of the IRA, and Early Literacy Consultant, Dallas, TX